Moniza Alvi was born in Pakistan and grew up in Hertfordshire. After working for many years as a secondary school teacher in London, she is now a freelance writer and tutor, and lives in Wymondham, Norfolk. Her first two collections were published by Oxford University Press, *The Country at My Shoulder* (1993), which was shortlisted for the T.S. Eliot and Whitbread poetry prizes, and *A Bowl of Warm Air* (1996).

Her later poetry titles have all been published by Bloodaxe: *Carrying My Wife* (2000), a Poetry Book Society Recommendation; *Souls* (2002); *How the Stone Found Its Voice* (2005); *Split World: Poems 1990-2005* (2008), which draws on all her previous books; and *Europa* (2008) and *At the Time of Partition* (2013), both these last two titles being Poetry Book Society Choices shortlisted for the T.S. Eliot Prize. She received a Cholmondeley Award in 2002. *Homesick for the Earth*, her versions of the French poet Jules Supervielle, was published by Bloodaxe Books in 2011.

MONIZA ALVI

AT THE TIME OF PARTITION

BLOODAXE BOOKS

ISBN: 978 1 85224 984 7

First published 2013 by
Bloodaxe Books Ltd,
Highgreen,
Tarset,
Northumberland NE48 1RP.

www.bloodaxebooks.com
For further information about Bloodaxe titles
please visit our website or write to
the above address for a catalogue.

Supported by
**ARTS COUNCIL
ENGLAND**

Cover design: Neil Astley & Pamela Robertson-Pearce.

Printed in Great Britain by Bell & Bain Limited, Glasgow, Scotland,
on acid-free paper sourced from mills with FSC chain of custody certification

At the Time of Partition is set during the time of the division of India in 1947. Inspired by family stories, it is a version of what might have taken place.

ACKNOWLEDGEMENTS

Thanks are due to the editors of the following publications where extracts from *At the Time of Partition* first appeared: *Exiled Ink, Ink Sweat and Tears, The London Magazine, Magma, Poetry International Web, Poetry London, Poetry Review* and *Vallum* (Canada). Excerpts will also appear in *Prairie Schooner* (USA).

Thank you to my writing friends for their invaluable assistance and encouragement. I am very grateful to Mara Bergman and Susan Wicks who read the manuscript.

I should like to pay tribute to Urvashi Butalia's *The Other Side of Silence: Voices from the Partition of India* (Hurst & Co., 2000), and also to Bapsi Sidhwa's novel set in Lahore at that time, *Ice-Candy-Man* (first published by William Heinemann Ltd in 1988).

'At This Time' was inspired by a line from a poem by Gellu Naum, and 'There but for the grace of Allah…' by a documentary photograph by Margaret Bourke-White.

And last, but not least, thank you to my family.

CONTENTS

At the Time of Partition

I began to realise that Partition was surely more than just a political divide, or a division of properties, of assets and liabilities. It was also, to use a phrase that survivors use repeatedly, a 'division of hearts'.

FROM Urvashi Butalia's *The Other Side of Silence: Voices from the Partition of India*

1 The Line

It lies helplessly, wrong side up
like a turtle showing its underside –

the family story. Is it there for the taking?

Can it be studied like life on a leaf
or under a stone?

Is it mine for the taking?

Like a conquered king,
the story limps away.

Pity the ending.
No story has an ending.

Attend the burial –
there will be a resurrection.

The stone rolls away
from the mouth of the cave.

*

Athar, my father's brother,
the young man with the damaged mind

who vanished,
simply went missing.

Over half a million lost their lives,
220,000 were declared missing.

Those were the official figures –
impossible to reckon the actual numbers.

*

Such a bright boy, they said.
But playing outside in the dust,

pushing a wheel in the dust one day.
One day – that sliver of time

in which anything can happen
and often doesn't,

but sometimes time takes one day
by the hand, or the scruff of the neck.

That day when any story
takes a deep breath

                    and begins –

*

The sun with its personal brightness
could only witness

the gay painted lorry
that struck him.

Quiet lunchtime, the shutters drawn
and it roared up

not in anger or indifference,
and dealt the small boy a blow

that blew him into another world.
A part of him had gone –

nobody wanted it
and yet it had been taken.

His father, himself a doctor
travelled
        far and wide,

took him to the best physicians –

*

In an exodus, such a child
grown up and not grown up

was ripe for being lost.

*

At the stroke of the midnight hour
when the world sleeps
India will awake to life and freedom.

Strong speech, yet fragile
as a bouquet

flung out to Delhi's
cheering oceanic crowds.

*

The midnight hour inched towards Nehru
as if it sensed its owner.

But my grandmother didn't own
the midnight hour –

widowed now, in Ludhiana,
a son in England,

five of her children
with their mother

on the wrong side of the line.

*

The window gaped, the plan was set:
Divide! Divide!

With four Muslims, four non-Muslims
Sir Cyril Radcliffe finalised the line.

He did it as fast as he was able, in the time
it takes to sort out a school timetable.

*

A line so delicate a sparrow might have
picked it up in its beak.

Not an artist's line, or a line of writing.

A line between birth and non-being.
A line that would mean death for so many.

The land itself at its calmest and most dignified
yielded to the line, lay still –

it didn't know what was coming.

India – and 'Pakistan':
the countries required their boundaries

as the thirsty needed water,
the beggars their begging bowls.

The line was its own religion,
it seemed to have its own God.

It sliced through a village, cut a house in half.
Where to place it in all of reality?

*

India will awake –
but for my grandmother

India draws away, irretrievably
like the tide going out.

2 Must We Go?

To place myself in my grandmother's shoes,
her chappals paired in the bedroom cool,

the mahogany dark,
lying by the prayer mat, facing Mecca,

awaiting her smaller, browner feet –
to plant my feet there,

or here, in a line of words
securely on the page.

*

To move house is one thing.
To leave your country another.

But to leave it
because it no longer wishes

to attach itself to you,
doesn't at all desire

to be the ground under your feet,
to feel compelled to leave it

for one which you had always known
to be a corner of your own,

but which has startlingly, deliriously
become another –

and which beckons
as if it had a hand to beckon with,

and which calls you,
as if a country had a single voice.

*

Amma they demand,
her protesting children.
Amma, must we go?

Can I take my cricket bat to Pakistan?
And what about school?

Only Athar has no questions.

*

The cards had been dealt
by a firm, if not a sure hand.

Ludhiana to India. West Punjab to Pakistan.
East Bengal to Pakistan.

Amritsar to India. Srinagar to India.
Lahore to Pakistan.

The Empire held fast like a sheet –
and shook out.

*

Doubt was an awkward thing –
there was no room for doubt.

At the margin of the great convulsion
her small household convulsed.

*

Pakistan was what it amounted to
                      Pakistan.

In the salting of lassi
in the knuckledents in dough
                      Pakistan.

In the pleating of a sari
in the sweeping of the hallway
                      Pakistan.

Between the question and its answer
                      Pakistan.

*

Rumours flew on the wind –
Nails of steel on the wind –

Infidels! Rapists!

Honour was the jewel,
not mother, sister.

To save their honour

bonfires were lit
and the women burned.

They asked me to do this,
but I ran away.
I couldn't set fire to my sister.

To protect their honour

ninety women jumped into a well.
There wasn't enough water
to drown them all.

*

And the rumour of a rumour

And the acting on a rumour

And the kernel of a rumour

*

The wisdom was to go.

Departure –
                the desperate,

the unimaginable thing

*

Already
her neighbourhood was emptying –
whole families had stolen away.

Which way to face?
She wrote to her son in England:

I pray for our safety at this time.
We will go by bus to Lahore.

3 Better By Far

By bus?

Better by far a magic carpet,
finely knotted, richer

than blood, broad enough
to keep the family together,

islanded, apart
from every danger,

journeying smoothly
across the unsegmented sky –

not in the cauldron of summer,
but in the fresher feel

of the last of winter,
the lucid mornings,

the greeny tinge
of the evening air,

Nehru to wave them on
and Jinnah to welcome them –

my grandmother, her pots and pans,
her lamp close by,

her parcels of layered clothes,
like mattresses,

Ahmed and Athar jostling for space,
Rahila, Jamila, Shehana,

the 'little' sisters,
a conspiracy of three,

with names, like mine
all ending in 'a', young girls,

cross-legged, daydreaming,
disentangling hello from goodbye.

4   Ever After

Ever after
she heard it as an echo

in her inner ear, disembodied,
as, in a sense, all voices are –

We'll take him, Shakira.
He can travel with us.

You've enough on your hands
with the other four.

There are places still
on the second bus, inshallah!

At that swollen moment
there was a shadowy unburdening

because at that time, perhaps
any child was a burden.

How she would wish
as the weeks and the months

and the lifetimes churned on
to undo *Take him,*

to force back the heavy, rusted
hands of the clock –

God's clock held by God's hands
in permanent view.

*

Say your goodbyes, ticked the clock.
No time to lose.

But who was left for goodbyes –
her Hindu friends, the friends of friends?

A stream drying up.

*

How to say it?
Tomorrow we will be gone.

It was hard to sit on a cane-seated chair
on her old veranda and sip tea,

the conversation curdling –
Tomorrow we will be gone.

The risk of departing
and the risk of remaining

weighing much the same.

*

Was the worst goodbye to the house?

The house was her second skin,
hardier than her first.

An island in the deafening,
tumultuous sea.

She was married to its daily rhythms –
the cleaning, kneading, praying...

Under duress,
it was dauntingly calm.

*

And Ludhiana itself, the Old City
and the New –

Civil Lines with its flowering trees.
The Christian Medical Hospital.

The cloth factories and the temples.
The neighbourliness of the lanes. Her lanes.

Bleeding internally, the city
tried to appear whole

for a final goodbye –

as *they* would gather and wait,
appear whole,

under Muslim rain and Hindu sun,
Hindu rain and Muslim sun.

*

Nothing was wrong with the clock.
The clock ticked on.

5 At This Time

With the loss of a husband,
friendship was a serious thing.

How to trust in friends,
to entrust to a friend,
or a friend of a friend,
at this time of fear – and hope?

Was a shaft of sunlight a friend?
Was a strand of cloud?

6 So They Took the Bus

which wasn't in any respect

a magic carpet –
though colours swirled

beneath the dirt on its sides.
It groaned and rattled

and smelled of pressed-in bodies
and garum masala and incense.

Did it smell more strongly
of the future or the past?

Would there ever be another day
as bland as a chapatti?

Would a day ever sing?

*

And Athar they enquired,
where is he?

He's with –
she explained it as best she could,

and peered through the grainy glass.

*

The bus was packed with single
and communal memories:

the unscrewing of a proud
nameplate from a wall,

the scrabbling of a wire-haired dog
on an empty porch,

the fervent embrace of an aunt
left behind.

*

Where will you live?
Have you any arrangements?

An arrangement?

It lay breathing at the end of the tunnel.

Hopped towards her like a tamed bird.

Like a kite, it tangled in the trees.

*

How much further? asked the children.
How much further? the adults asked of themselves.

Ludhiana to Lahore – not so very far.
But in Partition time...

*

At this point the back
of the story
            begins to break.

Can it walk at all?
Or hobble with a stick?

Will it close its eyes and drift into sleep?

How to serve it well?

A whole landscape to traverse –
and a modest page.

*

The night has half-smothered

its herons and geese
its vipers and cobras
its gently sloping plain
its rifles and swords

but it cannot smother
its stories:

the fruit vendor's tale, the farmer's tale,
the dark's own tales.

A train packed with the dead
and no young women among them.

Two sacks on board, filled
not with the curves of mangoes or melons,

but with women's breasts.

27

And that which should also never be known –

how, after decapitation
the hands will jerk upwards

above the stump of the neck,
have their last say.

Those tales

which had no beginnings
or had swallowed their endings,

tales which recoiled from
or feasted on themselves.

Who could rival the tales of the dark –
like Scheherazade
with no enchantment, no genie?

How to arrive at one overarching story?

*

A baby was born
in transit –
a stranger took a small dagger
from his belt
               and cut the cord

just like that.

*

Don't leave the bus
parents warned their children.

Better the airless bus
were the world entire.

7 Not the Thousand and One Nights

Not the thousand and one nights
but the thousand and one fears,

each one as full
as a night.

Fear stuck to the travellers,
and the travellers stuck to each other.

A single entity, a country in embryo
hurtling down the road,

its destination –
morning.

8 Stepping

We are lucky she thought.
Perhaps we are lucky.

'Lucky' as Nehru declared,
'to be stepping from the old to the new'.

'Stepping,' he'd said,
not 'trudging' or 'hurtling',

as if you took a calm footstep
and with less than the effort required

to leap into the air – you would leave
the old behind like a threadbare shawl

and immerse yourself in the new.
But could anywhere be new, that new?

Would the new-born Pakistan
be hoisted into being, like a flag?

Could she squeeze her familiar self
into one of its bright corners?

Ah, to be made new!
To be newly-made!

The morning was new
and these were morning thoughts.

The villages reduced to the howling of dogs
belonged to the night.

It was morning in her head,
morning in her stomach.

Soon – it would be afternoon.

9 *There but for the grace of Allah...*

Under the sparse shade
of a sparse tree
an old man lay dying
by the wayside, severed
from the moving world.
His wife fanned herself
with a tattered fan.
The grandchildren lolled.

What else was there to do

under the sparse shade
of a sparse tree,
the caravan gone?

10 No

No man's land, no woman's land.

    No food
    No water
    No dwellings
    No name.

Towns and villages
could scarcely be imagined.

A soul might shrivel away.

Oh to step down here into the dust
and stretch out

on an anonymous strip of land.
To refuse to move!

Would guards push her
across a hair's breadth line?

How did she come to be here
in a place so in love with no?

Where were the gatherings,
the family visits, the dressing up,

the tiny splendours
and consolations of the world?

Where was the world?
She could only gesture to where it might be.

They waited

between two lines of barbed wire
in a tide of buses and oxcarts.

But weren't they all Indians?

As yet
  Forever
      In a way...

11   The Camp

A vast parody of a city.

Almost featureless.
Teeming, but not bustling.

Children climbed trees
to see where the camp ended.

Tents – and patchwork shelters
of sheet metal, rags and bamboo.

Her temporary home, precarious
yet somehow enduring.

Ludhiana, a lifetime away.
Lahore, just out of reach.

Ragged ocean.
Oh to sail to the other side!

Where would they end up? And when?
And with what?

*

She washed fine-spun salwars,
hung them to dry wherever she could.

Queued for a bowl of flour,
two part-countries inside her.

Rahila, Jamila, Shehana
quarrelled in the cramped shelter,

or under the canopy of a walnut tree.
Carried water, swept the ground.

Cleaned their nails with twigs
to pass the time.

The nothingness was palpable –
you could pluck it from the air.

A boy took a message to the boundary line.
A daredevil pleasure.

Ahmed missed his older brothers:

Tariq in colder, safer
distant England –

Athar on the second bus,
soon to join them.

*

Holes in shelters
Holes in families

The losses
              trickled out,

poured out,

in the queues, in huddles
around the fire:

Father handed his wallet over.
Somebody hit him.
He bled to death.

Her eyes are sunken.
Her hands, withered.
A fishy smell.
The doctor says it's cholera.

Losses mounting on losses.

And the good fortune:

They warned us… They hid us…
Those angels sent from Allah!

*

The Housing Project – any news?

Any news? they demanded of each other,
of the police guards,
of the overarching sky.

Time flowered,
                    flowered and died.

*

And now, having come so far
I'll press on (as she couldn't press on)

and imagine it was here she found out
(indelibly here)

*

We're sorry they said,
the friends of friends.

So very sorry –

He isn't with us –

He disappeared at –

He vanished between –

The last time we saw him –

We did what we could –

Sorry. We're so very sorry.

*

And at dusk
his name sounded
in the mile-long roll call of the missing:

>   brothers
>   sons
>   aunts

fathers
daughters,
especially daughters

missing.

Deebas, Daras,
Kasheebas, Kalsooms,
Bhakirahs, Mairas, Baheras,
Yasmeenas, Mahruns...

Daughters missing.

And Athar – missing.

*

And there was forever someone
who thought they'd seen them
or knew someone, had a brother
or an uncle or a mother-in-law
who had seen, or had heard
   something –

seen Athar,
or someone just like him.

So you thought you saw him.
Where?
Tell me again.

*

Why did I..?

Why didn't they..?

A young man so doubly lost.

Knowing no better,
had he wandered off?

Would people be kind?

The darkness fell,
swooped, as darkness does.

12   Seeking

In God's name, where was he?
Amma, can we go and look?

*

Amma
climbed ridges, trailed a foot

along a valley floor,
laid the flat of her hand on a plain.

Her mind's eye was a torch
to beam through

the intricate darkness of a tailor's workshop,

the hanging, reeking bloodiness of a butcher's stall,

the forgotten corners of a woodcarver's yard.

   She'd glimpse his face

from a great height,
from alongside, from underneath,

find him squatting
at the back of a textile factory.

In an instant, he'd be gone.

*

India was behind her
as if somehow she'd outpaced it.

She had to turn around to see it
unroll,

or to watch it rise up
like a single mountain.

With a shake of her head she'd try
to clear a street,

sweep away the barriers
to seeing where he was.

*

Could anyone look as long and as hard as she did?

Not me, with my writing eye,

not in any crush of a bazaar, or wayside inn,
cranny, cleft in a rock.

Not with any muscle of the imagination.

13 Praying

She would build her house
out of prayer,

walk through the doorway
open the windows of prayer,

the solid home, the five-times-a-day
blessed regularity of prayer.

Athar had been dropped, wrenched
outside time,

but not beyond Allah's benevolence.

Allah, omnipotent, all-knowing and just –
surely He would listen, He would hear.

*

Allaahumma Salli ala Sayyidina Muhammadin...
O Allah, bless our Muhammad...

Sunrise. Noon. Mid-afternoon. Sunset. Nightfall.
Sunrise. Noon. Mid-afternoon. Sunset. Nightfall.

In the camp, the lifeline was prayer.

*

She made her *duas* – her intimate prayers,
prayer after prayer:

In the name of Allah,
the most merciful, the most compassionate...

Allah, where is my son?
Have pity on my son

I bow to You humbly
I ask for protection for my son

Allah, my son is missing
He isn't well – in his mind

14 On the Brink

The camp was on the brink of the city,
the city was on the brink of the camp.

The multitudes to be settled
waited to pour themselves

from one vessel to another,
to find their own level.

And the city itself began to lurch
from one entity to another,

to contend with the mass departure
of its Hindus and Sikhs,

to cope with the influx
of a million Muslim refugees.

Could it be as young and eager
as it was ravaged, old?

*

Only the sun rose every day
with no sense of loss –

overcame its spectacular death
of the evening before,

shone on the factories and printing presses,
the banks and transport companies,

the High Court and the Stock Exchange,
the GPO and the Provincial Assembly,

shone on Government College
and The Lady Mclagen Girls' High School,

on mosques, temples and gurdwaras,
on dense bazaars: Anarkali, Kashmiri...

on hovels and havelis,
on abandoned houses and gutted houses,

shone on all the worlds within worlds,
microcosms of the beleaguered,
                                        expectant city.

Lahore, still-beating heart of the Punjab.

15 And Now?

Brother,
            brother-in-England,

sister, sister, sister,

            mother –

the family
            began
                        to reconfigure

around an absence,
the ripeness
            of his loss.

Ripe, as if
            some fruit

must fall,

but hour by hour,
            month by month

no fruit fell.

*

No fruit,
but the offer of a house.

Or part of one. Not like for like –
the building shared,

no veranda, no garden with hibiscus
in a border, no almond trees.

A house, neither old nor new,
tucked away behind the bazaar,

leaning into a yellow courtyard,
its entrance on a narrow lane.

Amma, this will do!
Acha, acha... Yes... This will do...

*

They moved like trespassers
through the rooms of orphaned furniture,

claimed chests of drawers,
the shelves of the almirahs,

removed saris and underskirts,
sleeveless pullovers, shirts, salwars,

and replaced them with their own,
tried all the beds (were they softer, harder?)

inspected the kitchen, the bags of
lentils, flour, opened and unopened,

the tava in place on the stove,
waiting for the moons of roti,

and they noted in the darkened living-room
the number and position of chairs.

Everything as it was

when a family, mirroring their own
had grasped the future – and fled.

*

It was a day unlike any other,
though not a pigeon on a ledge,

not a dusty leaf,
knew it to be any different.

A roof over their heads!
It would do. Yes, it would do.

These rooms, though hushed
and yet-to-be-born,

reminded them of home.

*

Who lived here,
ate and slept, bore children?

The house in its inwardness
gave little away.

And who,

perhaps at this very hour,
were treading like burglars,

around the old Ludhiana home,
exclaiming at the garden, the veranda,

the bats and balls,
the set of 'Pocket Classics',

while agreeing that this lulled
and spacious house

would more than 'do' –
but hardly daring to think

that they could settle?

*

Don't look back –
that's what people said.

But these very words
could prompt her to turn around
                                    sharply,

to try to glimpse
what was happening all those miles

behind her,
and to say another goodbye.

And where would anyone be
without memory?

We have survived people said,
though whole chunks were missing.

*

And I,

in my presumption,
have brought them here

    a second time –

as if, in this instance
I'm accompanying them

like someone from The Housing Project
who they'd rather wasn't there,

showing them this house
in the quiet of its abandonment,

pointing out the courtyard
with its square of blue sky.

16 Settling

It would take time.
Of course. Of course.

Forwards, backwards,
time lost itself in alleyways,

or stood still, trapped
like water in the Lahore Canal.

The Mall, Temple Road,
the Railway Station –

everywhere seemed to soak up time.
Yet minute by minute, month by month,

just as they did,
Pakistan grew steadily older.

Divided as it was into East and West,
divided and subdivided,

it had heaved itself out of a giant egg –
to have birthdays.

It was one year old. Two years old.
It was remarkably new,

and quick to age.
And always there was India,

its immense shadow,
forever fixed to its heels.

*

To settle – with a son missing?

Was it better to think of him
alive or dead?

Impossible not to think of him.

She appealed and appealed
to the authorities – as did so many.

Sent out messages
by word of mouth.

She kept on searching –
she was covered in eyes.

Still he was missing –

sometimes plainly in front of her
but never within reach.

And she would begin
the complicated interlacing

of forgetting and remembering.

But then –
there was no such thing as to forget.

*

Settle, in a sense, they did,
like pebbles dropped into the city.

Settle with the old friends. And the new.
The family across the lane

who owned a shoe factory:
The best chappals – please, you choose!

Slowly they slipped
into the folds of the neighbourhood.

*

Day by day the city, the country
became more securely theirs.

It was resolutely Pakistan.
It was scarcely Pakistan.

She could turn a corner
and think *This is India!*

The India it had assuredly been
not so very long ago.

And yet, and yet –
the newness, the flavour of Pakistan.

*

The newness. And the rawness.
The rawness of her loss.

Before all this
she had lost a husband.

And then a home,
                    a homeland –

and now a son.

Such a bright boy.
Twice lost.

And she had gained –

there was no certainty.

Pakistan.

The flames had died down.
Or had they?

Pakistan.

A country was too large a place
to contemplate.

17 And Where?

Pakistan! the crowd roared.
Pakistan Zindabad! Long live Pakistan!

This country – her country.
A nation in its instability,

one that could change lives
with the suddenness of a blow to the head.

And Jinnah – his photograph was everywhere,
in the newspaper, on crumbling walls.

Jinnah, in his elegant Western-style suit.
As handsome as Nehru, she thought,

but too thin. He was ill –
some said he was dying.

Jinnah who'd had his doubts,
had once striven for unity,

but now stood supreme,
the Father of the Nation

proposing
>   *A State in which we could live and breathe*
>   *as free men...*

Mohammed Ali Jinnah. And her lost son.
At rest in the afternoon, or on waking

she might picture them both,
one superimposed on the other.

*

Her country, and the other. The border
tantalisingly close.

At first easy to cross, no passports required.
Then increasingly hard.

The ever-disputed border.

18   Partition of Hearts

They called it the Partition of Hearts,
this dark side of Independence.

Blame the British, blame Congress,
blame Nehru, blame Jinnah.

But what was the point?

They called it the Partition of Hearts.

Yet connections had not been broken,
not quite –

between Pakistan and India
                    the living and the dead
the families and the missing
                    the people and themselves.

They called it the Partition of Hearts –
this Partition of reinforced glass.

19   Continuing

She made paneer in her kitchen
in their half of the house,

strained milk through a muslin bag
to separate the curd from the whey.

There was help with the housework –
Alice, a girl from the Christian Mission.

There were gatherings, as of old,
of family and friends,

and the exchange of news.
News. And no news.

*

We are here she said –
and the being here

was both half-familiar
and remote as the Himalayas.

There was school for Ahmed,
school for Rahila, Jamila and Shehana.

Pride and Prejudice,
                    Great Expectations,

and novels by Thomas Hardy
where everything seemed to be doomed.

And cricket was played.
Remember the old Ludhiana days

with a kerosene drum for a wicket.
Bang! And you were out.

Remember they said,
remember Anwar and Iqbal,

their guava trees,
their horse-drawn carriage...

As for her own family land –
a small piece was given in lieu.

*

What was there to cling to
but hope?

The fine escarpment of hope.

Hope in her children,
her sons – her daughters.

Hope in the future, of some vestige
of the-past-in-the-future.

Hope – and human warmth.

*

Her son would return from England

with his English wife (tall and green-eyed)
and she might give birth to a child –

the solid embodiment of hope?

And they might stay –
who could know?

Nothing was certain.

20 Crossing Back

The line between birth and non-being.

The line between what happened
and the imagining.

A line so delicate a sparrow might have
picked it up in its beak.

A line of writing.

A line so definite –
and so blurred.

*

Time to return the unending story
to itself.

Time to return everyone
to themselves.

Time to cross swiftly back

over the line.